The DEFINITIVE guide to Trump's Hate-Filled Racist Remarks

2020 Election Special Edition

By Kamala Warren

ISBN: 978-0-9853449-8-6

Cover image by janeb13 on Pixabay.com

Disclaimer: After carrying out untold hours of exhaustive investigation with the intent of providing a definitive guide on the subject, it is to the best of the author's knowledge that all of the information presented in this is book is both accurate and properly attributed – hence, all of the pages are blank.

Saint Grobian Press

Sacramento – Trenton – Utica – Portland – Inverness - Dayton

Check out our other great products at:

www.UnionOfTruth.org

Other books by Kamala Warren:

1- The DEFINITIVE Guide to Facts and Logic that Justify the Mandatory Usage of Preferred Pronouns

2- The DEFINITIVE Guide to Facts and Logic that Justify Disarming Law-Abiding Citizens

3- The DEFINITIVE Guide to Fact-based Justification for Trump's Impeachment

4- The DEFINITIVE Guide to Facts and Logic that Justify Sanctuary Cities

5- The DEFINITIVE Guide to Facts and Logic that Justify Universal Basic Income

6- The DEFINITIVE Guide to Trump's Treasonous Collusion and Obstruction

7- The DEFINITIVE Guide to Fact-based Justification for Homosexual Indoctrination of Kindergarten Students

8- The DEFINITIVE Guide to Fact-based Justification for Spying on Candidate Trump

9- The DEFINITIVE Guide to Democratic Party Accomplishments in the Trump Era

10- The DEFINITIVE Guide to Cogent Liberal Talking Points

11- The DEFINITIVE Guide to Facts and Logic that Justify Government-Run Healthcare

The DEFINITIVE guide to Trump's Hate-Filled Racist
Remarks

The DEFINITIVE guide to Trump's Hate-Filled Racist
Remarks

The DEFINITIVE guide to Trump's Hate-Filled Racist
Remarks

The DEFINITIVE guide to Trump's Hate-Filled Racist
Remarks

The DEFINITIVE guide to Trump's Hate-Filled Racist
Remarks

The DEFINITIVE guide to Trump's Hate-Filled Racist
Remarks

The DEFINITIVE guide to Trump's Hate-Filled Racist
Remarks

The DEFINITIVE guide to Trump's Hate-Filled Racist
Remarks

The DEFINITIVE guide to Trump's Hate-Filled Racist
Remarks

The DEFINITIVE guide to Trump's Hate-Filled Racist
Remarks

The DEFINITIVE guide to Trump's Hate-Filled Racist
Remarks

The DEFINITIVE guide to Trump's Hate-Filled Racist Remarks

The DEFINITIVE guide to Trump's Hate-Filled Racist
Remarks

The DEFINITIVE guide to Trump's Hate-Filled Racist
Remarks

The DEFINITIVE guide to Trump's Hate-Filled Racist
Remarks

The DEFINITIVE guide to Trump's Hate-Filled Racist
Remarks

The DEFINITIVE guide to Trump's Hate-Filled Racist
Remarks

The DEFINITIVE guide to Trump's Hate-Filled Racist
Remarks

The DEFINITIVE guide to Trump's Hate-Filled Racist
Remarks

The DEFINITIVE guide to Trump's Hate-Filled Racist
Remarks

The DEFINITIVE guide to Trump's Hate-Filled Racist
Remarks

The DEFINITIVE guide to Trump's Hate-Filled Racist
Remarks

The DEFINITIVE guide to Trump's Hate-Filled Racist
Remarks

The DEFINITIVE guide to Trump's Hate-Filled Racist
Remarks

The DEFINITIVE guide to Trump's Hate-Filled Racist
Remarks

The DEFINITIVE guide to Trump's Hate-Filled Racist
Remarks

The DEFINITIVE guide to Trump's Hate-Filled Racist
Remarks

The DEFINITIVE guide to Trump's Hate-Filled Racist
Remarks

The DEFINITIVE guide to Trump's Hate-Filled Racist
Remarks

The DEFINITIVE guide to Trump's Hate-Filled Racist
Remarks

The DEFINITIVE guide to Trump's Hate-Filled Racist
Remarks

The DEFINITIVE guide to Trump's Hate-Filled Racist
Remarks

The DEFINITIVE guide to Trump's Hate-Filled Racist
Remarks

The DEFINITIVE guide to Trump's Hate-Filled Racist
Remarks

The DEFINITIVE guide to Trump's Hate-Filled Racist
Remarks

The DEFINITIVE guide to Trump's Hate-Filled Racist
Remarks

The DEFINITIVE guide to Trump's Hate-Filled Racist
Remarks

The DEFINITIVE guide to Trump's Hate-Filled Racist Remarks

The DEFINITIVE guide to Trump's Hate-Filled Racist
Remarks

The DEFINITIVE guide to Trump's Hate-Filled Racist
Remarks

The DEFINITIVE guide to Trump's Hate-Filled Racist
Remarks

The DEFINITIVE guide to Trump's Hate-Filled Racist
Remarks

The DEFINITIVE guide to Trump's Hate-Filled Racist
Remarks

The DEFINITIVE guide to Trump's Hate-Filled Racist
Remarks

The DEFINITIVE guide to Trump's Hate-Filled Racist
Remarks

The DEFINITIVE guide to Trump's Hate-Filled Racist
Remarks

The DEFINITIVE guide to Trump's Hate-Filled Racist
Remarks

The DEFINITIVE guide to Trump's Hate-Filled Racist Remarks

The DEFINITIVE guide to Trump's Hate-Filled Racist
Remarks

The DEFINITIVE guide to Trump's Hate-Filled Racist
Remarks

The DEFINITIVE guide to Trump's Hate-Filled Racist
Remarks

The DEFINITIVE guide to Trump's Hate-Filled Racist
Remarks

The DEFINITIVE guide to Trump's Hate-Filled Racist
Remarks

The DEFINITIVE guide to Trump's Hate-Filled Racist
Remarks

The DEFINITIVE guide to Trump's Hate-Filled Racist
Remarks

The DEFINITIVE guide to Trump's Hate-Filled Racist
Remarks

The DEFINITIVE guide to Trump's Hate-Filled Racist
Remarks

The DEFINITIVE guide to Trump's Hate-Filled Racist
Remarks

The DEFINITIVE guide to Trump's Hate-Filled Racist
Remarks

The DEFINITIVE guide to Trump's Hate-Filled Racist
Remarks

The DEFINITIVE guide to Trump's Hate-Filled Racist
Remarks

The DEFINITIVE guide to Trump's Hate-Filled Racist
Remarks

The DEFINITIVE guide to Trump's Hate-Filled Racist
Remarks

The DEFINITIVE guide to Trump's Hate-Filled Racist
Remarks

The DEFINITIVE guide to Trump's Hate-Filled Racist
Remarks

The DEFINITIVE guide to Trump's Hate-Filled Racist
Remarks

The DEFINITIVE guide to Trump's Hate-Filled Racist
Remarks

The DEFINITIVE guide to Trump's Hate-Filled Racist
Remarks

The DEFINITIVE guide to Trump's Hate-Filled Racist
Remarks

The DEFINITIVE guide to Trump's Hate-Filled Racist
Remarks

The DEFINITIVE guide to Trump's Hate-Filled Racist
Remarks

The DEFINITIVE guide to Trump's Hate-Filled Racist
Remarks

The DEFINITIVE guide to Trump's Hate-Filled Racist
Remarks

The DEFINITIVE guide to Trump's Hate-Filled Racist
Remarks

The DEFINITIVE guide to Trump's Hate-Filled Racist
Remarks

The DEFINITIVE guide to Trump's Hate-Filled Racist
Remarks

The DEFINITIVE guide to Trump's Hate-Filled Racist
Remarks

The DEFINITIVE guide to Trump's Hate-Filled Racist
Remarks

The DEFINITIVE guide to Trump's Hate-Filled Racist
Remarks

The DEFINITIVE guide to Trump's Hate-Filled Racist
Remarks

The DEFINITIVE guide to Trump's Hate-Filled Racist
Remarks

The DEFINITIVE guide to Trump's Hate-Filled Racist
Remarks

The DEFINITIVE guide to Trump's Hate-Filled Racist
Remarks

The DEFINITIVE guide to Trump's Hate-Filled Racist
Remarks

The DEFINITIVE guide to Trump's Hate-Filled Racist
Remarks

The DEFINITIVE guide to Trump's Hate-Filled Racist
Remarks

The DEFINITIVE guide to Trump's Hate-Filled Racist
Remarks

The DEFINITIVE guide to Trump's Hate-Filled Racist
Remarks

The DEFINITIVE guide to Trump's Hate-Filled Racist
Remarks

The DEFINITIVE guide to Trump's Hate-Filled Racist
Remarks

The DEFINITIVE guide to Trump's Hate-Filled Racist
Remarks

The DEFINITIVE guide to Trump's Hate-Filled Racist
Remarks

The DEFINITIVE guide to Trump's Hate-Filled Racist
Remarks

The DEFINITIVE guide to Trump's Hate-Filled Racist
Remarks

The DEFINITIVE guide to Trump's Hate-Filled Racist
Remarks

The DEFINITIVE guide to Trump's Hate-Filled Racist
Remarks

www.ingramcontent.com/pod-product-compliance
Lightning Source LLC
Chambersburg PA
CBHW051001050726
47592CB00007B/2664